HOW SHOULD I
MANAGE TIME?

✘ CULTIVATING BIBLICAL GODLINESS

Series Editors

Joel R. Beeke and Ryan M. McGraw

Dr. D. Martyn Lloyd-Jones once said that what the church needs to do most of all is "to begin herself to live the Christian life. If she did that, men and women would be crowding into our buildings. They would say, 'What is the secret of this?'" As Christians, one of our greatest needs is for the Spirit of God to cultivate biblical godliness in us in order to put the beauty of Christ on display through us, all to the glory of the triune God. With this goal in mind, this series of booklets treats matters vital to Christian experience at a basic level. Each booklet addresses a specific question in order to inform the mind, warm the affections, and transform the whole person by the Spirit's grace, so that the church may adorn the doctrine of God our Savior in all things.

HOW SHOULD I
MANAGE TIME?

RYAN M. MCGRAW

REFORMATION HERITAGE BOOKS
GRAND RAPIDS, MICHIGAN

How Should I Manage Time?
© 2016 by Ryan M. McGraw

All rights reserved. No part of this book may be used or reproduced in any manner whatsoever without written permission except in the case of brief quotations embodied in critical articles and reviews. Direct your requests to the publisher at the following address:

Reformation Heritage Books
2965 Leonard St. NE
Grand Rapids, MI 49525
616-977-0889 / Fax 616-285-3246
orders@heritagebooks.org
www.heritagebooks.org

Printed in the United States of America
16 17 18 19 20 21/10 9 8 7 6 5 4 3 2 1

ISBN 978-1-60178-469-8

For additional Reformed literature, request a free book list from Reformation Heritage Books at the above regular or e-mail address.

HOW SHOULD I
MANAGE TIME?
―――――✗―――――

When I was a young Christian and a college student, a sermon by Jonathan Edwards (1703–1758) caught my eye. The title was "Procrastination." Since college students are prone to procrastination in their studies, I decided that I wanted to know what Edwards had to say on the subject. I was surprised to find that this was a message on why coming to Christ is an urgent necessity and why people should come to Him without delay. The preceding sermon in the volume, "On the Preciousness of Time," was to the same effect.

What does this have to do with how we must live as godly Christians and how we think about time management? The point of convergence is that our prospect of eternity radically alters our attitude toward time. If we do not see the urgency of coming to Christ, then we are, by definition, wasting our time and our lives. Conversely, when we come to the Father, through Jesus Christ, by the work of the Spirit in our hearts, this should transform how we use our time. Time management is important for

Christians because only Christians can begin to use time well.

In Ephesians 5:16, the apostle Paul describes Christians as "redeeming the time, because the days are evil." In the context, the teaching of this passage engulfs and consumes every duty of the Christian life. How you use your time is the measure of the quality of your life. This booklet aims to show that we must manage our time well in order to serve the Lord and His church well. The issue of time management raises one caution and two questions. The caution is that, as John Murray wrote, "the line of demarcation between virtue and vice is not a chasm but a razor's edge."[1] This is true of time management as well as every area of personal holiness. The two questions are "What is Paul teaching Christians about time?" and "How does this affect my life?" These two questions will draw out the implications of Paul's teaching in the text and show how time management is a significant aspect of the Christian life.

WHAT IS PAUL TEACHING CHRISTIANS ABOUT TIME MANAGEMENT?

Managing time is the same as managing anything else. No one moves up into a management position without the knowledge and experience needed to qualify them for management. In order to use

---

1. John Murray, *Principles of Conduct: Aspects of Christian Ethics* (Grand Rapids: Eerdmans, 1957), 56.

time well as a Christian, you must first know what it means to be a Christian and to have the experience of knowing God. Such knowledge transforms every moment of time in this world. We will see how Paul lays this foundation for us by a brief survey of Ephesians and then narrow our focus to the specific characteristics and qualifications of one who can manage time well. This will demonstrate how Christ transforms our use of time.

A Gospel Foundation for Time Management: The Context of Ephesians

Every aspect of Christian living must begin with the glory of the triune God and the work of the Father, the Son, and the Spirit in salvation. This is even more immediately apparent in the book of Ephesians than in other parts of the New Testament.

Paul begins by expounding the glory of the gospel in terms of the glorious work of the Father, the Son, and the Holy Spirit. The Father blesses believers in Christ because He chose them in Him before the foundation of the world (1:3–4). He adopts believers into His family through Christ (1:5), gives them a heavenly inheritance (1:18), and raises them from spiritual death and seats them in heaven with Him even while they live on earth (2:6).

The Son redeems believers from sin through His blood, forgives them in His rich and abounding grace, and reveals the Father's eternal wisdom in planning their salvation (1:7–10). Christ makes people alive who were dead in trespasses and sins (2:5), reconciles people to God and to each other (2:11–22), and communicates to them His love, which passes knowledge (3:19).

The Holy Spirit is the seal that believers belong to God and is the down payment of the inheritance that believers have from the Father through the Son (1:13–14). He is a seal by placing God's stamp of ownership on them. He is a down payment because those who have fellowship with Him have fellowship with the triune Lord of heaven. Through His power, Christians begin to live as citizens of heaven.

Like a compact jewel in a prominent display case, Ephesians 2:18 summarizes the glorious work of the triune God: "For through him [Christ] we both have access by one Spirit unto the Father." All people from all nations and cultures, whether Jews or Gentiles, have the same access to God when they come to the Father, through His Son, and by His Spirit. God does all this "to the praise of the glory of his grace" (1:6; see also vv. 12, 14). The Christian life is based on the work of the triune God, and Christian living is the outworking of communion with the triune God through union with Christ.

Ephesians 4:1 introduces Christian living as it is based on the glorious gospel foundation of chapters 1–3. Paul writes, "I therefore, the prisoner of the Lord, beseech you that ye walk worthy of the vocation wherewith ye are called." This is the context where the exhortation to redeem the time appears

(5:16). Walking worthy of our calling in Christ ("vocation") means living together in the church faithfully (4:2–16), developing habits of personal godliness in specific ways (4:17–5:21), and establishing gospel-shaped family relationships (5:22–6:9).

Many people want to skip doctrine and principles in order to move on to lists of what they must do. However, unless you begin with Paul's trinitarian gospel, then time management cannot help you. You can be industrious with your time whether you are a Christian or not. Christians can learn from non-Christians how to make schedules and to work hard. But if you do not know God, then what will you have to show from your skill in time management? What can it profit you if you gain the whole world yet lose your own soul (Mark 8:36)? Time management is an all-or-nothing endeavor. Regardless of what you do with your time each day, you will either gain all of your time at once or lose it all at once. Everything that you do will either be in vain or be done with the purpose, drive, and joy that can come only to those who know the Father, through the Son, by the Spirit. Will you not come to Christ today? Will you read Ephesians and understand His gospel better? If you do not begin with this foundation, then may the Spirit not allow you to read further until He drives you to the foot of the cross! Only then can you begin to spend time wisely to enjoy life properly.

Be Careful How You Live: The Context of Ephesians 5:15–21

What does Paul mean by redeeming the time? The full sentence in which this text is contained says, "See then that ye walk circumspectly, not as fools, but as wise, redeeming the time, because the days are evil" (Eph. 5:15–16). This is an exhortation to be careful how you live. It serves as a transition from the preceding to the following sections of the book. The basic idea is, as Peter O'Brien put it, "Those who are *wise* will have a right attitude to time."[2]

In colloquial English, we use the expression "to buy time." The Greek Septuagint translation of Daniel 2:8 uses precisely this expression to describe the Babylonian magicians and fortune tellers buying time when the king threatened to kill them. "Buying time" refers to postponing an anticipated outcome, usually with the desire to change the results. Paul is not telling us to buy time to avoid the future. He is using a metaphor that encompasses every second of every day. As O'Brien concludes, "Believers will act wisely by snapping up every opportunity that comes."[3] This does not mean using every opportunity for self-preservation, as the magicians in Daniel 2:8, nor for our financial gain or comfort, as the rest of the world. We must make the most of every

---

2. Peter O'Brien, *Ephesians* (Grand Rapids: Eerdmans, 1991), 382 (emphasis original).

3. O'Brien, *Ephesians*, 382.

moment of every day—morning, noon, and night—to glorify God and to serve Him and His church.

The reason enforcing this command makes it urgent: "because the days are evil." Scripture frequently characterizes the present state of the world as evil. Galatians 1:4 describes Christ saving us "from this present evil world" according to the will of our God and Father. First John 5:19 adds that "we are of God, and the whole world lieth in wickedness." There is a time of glory coming in a new heaven and new earth in which righteousness dwells, but that time is not now. When we enter into glory, we will know that the sufferings of this life were not worthy of comparison to it (Rom. 8:18). God is good and does good (Ps. 119:68); we must imitate Him as dearly beloved children (Eph. 5:1). The world will not encourage us to seek God and to do good. Failing to retain God in its thinking is what makes this world evil (Rom. 1:28) and what makes it dangerous to us.

It is as though Paul is saying that Christians should remember that they have a short time to do good in a fallen, evil world. Christians are the only ones who have the potential to use time well because they are the only ones who live and die for the glory of the triune God. The world is passing away together with its lusts, but he who does the will of God will abide forever (1 John 2:17). A wise Christian has one eye on the clock and one eye on Christ's second coming. We must labor wisely for the glory of God now because a time is coming in which no one can work (John 9:4).

In order to redeem the time, we must know what the will of the Lord is. Ephesians 5:17–21 explains, in part, what this looks like:

> Wherefore be ye not unwise, but understanding what the will of the Lord is. And be not drunk with wine, wherein is excess; but be filled with the Spirit; speaking to yourselves in psalms and hymns and spiritual songs, singing and making melody in your heart to the Lord; giving thanks always for all things unto God and the Father in the name of our Lord Jesus Christ; submitting yourselves one to another in the fear of God.

These characteristics underscore the duties listed in chapters 4 and 5, and they prepare for the family and work relations treated in chapters 5 and 6. In other words, being filled with the Spirit is a description of knowing God's will, singing praises to Him, giving thanks in all things, and preferring one another before ourselves (Phil. 2:3) in every relationship and labor of life, all because we fear God.

Christians must be thoughtful and purposeful about their use of time. Unplanned time is wasted time. If we do not carry with us a sense of the preciousness of time, then we will not promote Christ's kingdom or do good to others. Worse still, we will serve Satan's kingdom by making the evil days worse. Redeeming the time is the great means in this passage through which we channel all of the duties of the Christian life in love and gratitude to Christ, by the help of the Holy Spirit, to the glory of God.

How Christ Redeems Our Time and Why It Should Be Precious to Us

We can redeem the time because Christ has already redeemed our lives and our time. You can make the most of time because Christ has made it possible for you to glorify and enjoy God forever. If you are not reconciled to God through Christ, and God is not your Father, then what will you gain from your labors and efforts? It is vain for you to rise early and to stay up late (Ps. 127:2). Will not your time rise up as a witness against you on the day of judgment? The time that you used and spent for your own profit, enjoyment, and gain will testify against you in the presence of believers. They will receive everlasting profit and enjoyment and gain when they see Christ in His unveiled glory. Christ redeemed our time by redeeming us from sin. He covers all of our abuses of time with His own precious blood, and God looks on us as though we had used every second for His glory. He looks at us through the lens of the righteous Savior, who never wasted a second of His time.

This does not mean that we do not need to use our time well. Christ makes our time sacred so that we may consecrate it joyfully to His service. Wasting or misspending time is sinful. It is a privilege to use our time well because there is no condemnation to those who are in Christ Jesus (Rom. 8:1) and because we bear His name in this world. The Savior gives to us His Spirit (1 John 4:13). The Spirit aims to make us like Christ by making us holy in Christ. After God removes our guilt and constitutes us righteous through uniting us to Christ's life and death, the Spirit tinctures our character with Christ's righteous character. As Christ was raised to walk in newness of life, so the Spirit unites us to Christ in His resurrection so that we can walk in newness of life (Rom. 6:1–4).

He will complete this process only when we see Christ face-to-face in heaven (1 John 3:2). In the meantime, this transforms how we use our time in this world. Time is life. He who uses his time well lives his life well. This places our use of time in a positive light. To the unbeliever, the passing of time is a great tragedy, adding to his condemnation. To the believer, every moment of time is an opportunity, adding to an eternal weight of glory. Time provides opportunity to hallow God the Father through a holy and reverent use of all things through which He makes Himself known.

Time should be precious to us. It is something that we can spend but never replenish. When we spend our money, we go back to work and earn more. We put some of it in bank accounts and invest some of it in order to gain interest. Yet with regard to time, the Lord has given us an immutable lump sum for us to invest. What we spend is gone, never to return. We spend some of this lump sum every second of every day. Should this not make you consider carefully how you use your time? Let us gain interest on this valuable commodity, using those talents that the Lord has committed to our trust, aiming to hear Him say, "Well done, good and faithful servant…enter thou into the joy of thy lord" (Matt. 25:23).

WHAT DOES THIS MEAN FOR MY LIFE?

Now that we understand the biblical principles of the value of time, we can consider how to manage our time in a God-honoring way. We must distinguish between principles derived from Scripture, the fact that we *must* apply them, and the varied ways in which we *may* apply them. For example, we must meditate daily on the Word of God (Ps. 1:2). We may do this by prayerfully reading through the entire Bible in a year or through some other method. We may read at different times of the day and more at some times than others. Similarly, using time well means being intentional with how we use time.

We must beware simultaneously of overscheduling our time and undervaluing it. My wife and I have read several books on homemaking. Some of these books try to impose an inflexible self-legislature on how we use every minute of every day. This approach often leads to discouragement. Rarely does it lead to using time as joyful service to God and others. Many react to this approach and swing to the opposite extreme and give little thought to how they use time. These people accomplish much less than they could with a bit of prayerful planning. We need examples to help structure our time and use it well to the glory of the triune God. How we do so will vary widely from person to person, and we must exercise much charity in this regard. The following directions are designed to help you think through biblical principles and develop your own application from them.

Be Intentional in Using Time

A presbytery in which I served required interns to keep track of everything they did for every hour of the day for one week. The purpose of this exercise was not to teach interns how to create a schedule but how to become aware of what they are doing currently. The results were almost unanimous. Almost every intern became aware of how much time he was losing each day. If we are not intentional with our time, then we will lose our time.

This does not mean that we must devote all our time to work. Ecclesiastes 3:1–8 says,

> To every thing there is a season, and a time to every purpose under the heaven: a time to be born, and a time to die; a time to plant, and a time to pluck up that which is planted; a time to kill, and a time to heal; a time to break down, and a time to build up; a time to weep, and a time to laugh; a time to mourn, and a time to dance; a time to cast away stones, and a time to gather stones together; a time to embrace, and a time to refrain from embracing; a time to get, and a time to lose; a time to keep, and a time to cast away;

> a time to rend, and a time to sew; a time to keep silence, and a time to speak; a time to love, and a time to hate; a time of war, and a time of peace.

There is a time for work and there is a time for rest and recreation. We can dishonor God by working without rest or exercise just as much as we can by resting and exercising without working. The key to learning how to redeem the time is learning how to hold every activity of life in proper proportion, to know what is appropriate for what occasion, and to do it all to the glory of the triune God. Though applied to a particular problem regarding eating meat offered to idols, this principle stands behind Paul's exhortation, "Whether therefore ye eat, or drink, or whatsoever ye do, do all to the glory of God" (1 Cor. 10:31). Before considering what to do with your time, you must think through how and why you are using your time.

Learn to Prioritize Your Projects

A friend tells a story about a wealthy businessman who noticed that one of his employees was unusually productive. When he asked the man what his secret was, he replied that he would tell him, but that, in exchange, he should try his method for a month and then write him a check for what he thought it was worth. The principle was to make a list of pending projects and to prioritize them in order of importance. If at all possible, do not go to number 2 on the list until number 1 is complete. The same procedure applies to the remaining items on this list, constantly reevaluating what was most important. The wealthy businessman tried this for one month and then promptly wrote the man a check for $10,000. In a Christian context, this not only means reevaluating priorities but sometimes repenting of misplaced priorities. The point is to be thoughtful and intentionally drive toward those areas of life that are most important. It is helpful to prioritize and to reprioritize your projects.

Learn to Combine Projects When Possible
As a busy minister, I have learned to develop a prayerful creativity in incorporating books, articles, reviews, conferences, and other projects into the centrality of the ministry of the local church. This is always a learning curve and does not always work out as planned, but it is the only way to attempt to expand my labors as far and wide as possible. For example, I preached a sermon series on the gospel of John. At the same time, I worked on my doctoral project, which treats John Owen's practical use of the doctrine of the Trinity and public worship. The gospel of John reveals more about the triunity of God than any other book of Scripture. This meant that reading Owen and other Puritan and Reformed authors on this subject gave me a wealth of material to weave into my preaching and sermon application. The sermons were richer for it.

At the same time, I taught a Sunday school course on the sacraments. Since my research included public worship, I drew from this material extensively to improve the class. During this time, I spoke about Owen on the Holy Spirit at one conference, preached two sermons on the Trinity and the Christian ministry at another, and wrote a popular book to make this material accessible to the average person in the church. I also wrote book reviews to help me solidify what I was reading and to digest it prayerfully until it became a part of my own piety and preaching. This had both immediate and long-term effects on my ministry.

This example may appear complex, but it was an answer to fervent prayer that the Lord would give wisdom to bless everything that I read, preached, and wrote for the good of the church. This is more of an example of the Lord's faithfulness in answering prayer than it is of personal ingenuity and creative planning. The Holy Spirit is able to expand our use of these principles beyond our natural ability.

Learning to combine projects or profitable activities applies to every other area of life as well. A homemaker can listen to sermons while preparing meals through the use of modern technology. She can teach children to learn how to work hard for God's glory by involving them in household chores, such as folding laundry. Such activities create opportunities to engage children in fruitful conversation during the daily affairs of life. This is a means of teaching them when we sit down, and rise up, and walk by the wayside (Deut. 6:7; 11:19).

Men can spend quality time with their children by taking them along on a trip to the hardware store or even on a business trip. How we redeem the time by combining activities is limited only by our creative imaginations.

Avoid Overscheduling Your Day

Few things are as discouraging as never finishing our essential priorities day after day. Assume that the tasks on your calendar will take longer than you think they will, and plan to accomplish less. Being intentional with how you use time and learning how to prioritize can help you with this. Set small and reasonable goals. Sometimes prioritizing does not mean literally finishing one thing on a list and then moving to the next until you have finished everything. It may mean making one large priority for specific days of the week. For example, one homemaking book mentions setting apart a laundry day, a cooking day, an office day to pay bills, and so on.[4] "Cooking day" may involve making meals and food that a family can use for several days. It may also be helpful for some people to take time to plan a menu for the rest of the week. These categories are not absolute. A child spilling food on several pairs of clothes may require more laundry on cooking day.

---

4. Kim Brenneman, *Large Family Logistics: The Art and Science of Managing the Large Family* (San Antonio, Tex.: The Vision Forum, 2010).

Learn your limitations. A schedule is a servant. Do not turn it into a master. If you cannot do everything that is on your list that day, then the Lord has not called you to do everything that you think you need to do. This is a good opportunity to reassess your priorities. It is better for morale to underschedule than to overschedule the day. You will always have other things that you want to do, and you can work them in if you finish early what you need to do. Be encouraged as well that gifts and abilities are not a static reality. The Lord increases gifts and graces when we use them faithfully. Reading books enables you to read better and to read (and remember) more books. Redeeming the time is like building a muscle. You must develop it through exercise, and you must begin with light weights rather than heavy ones.

Learn to Enjoy Today's Work

We can redeem the time only if we enjoy the work that God has given us to do today. Ecclesiastes 3:22 says, "Wherefore I perceive that there is nothing better, than that a man should rejoice in his own works; for that is his portion: for who shall bring him to see what shall be after him?" Enjoying our work is a gift from God. Our work does and should occupy most of our time in an ordinary week. We must learn to enjoy our work even when our work is not enjoyable. We must enjoy work because it is the gift of God and because we do it to the Lord and not to men. In the providence of God, the work that we do today may be the only work that we ever have the opportunity to do.

A young man can sift through filthy clothes all day at a dry cleaners to the glory of God when he redeems the time by doing so. A woman can change diapers all day, clean a seemingly uncleanable house, and do numerous other mundane tasks, all to the glory of God. If we do these things cheerfully to the Lord and seek to honor Him with the time that we spend on them, then we can glorify and enjoy Him as much as those who are devoted to full-time Christian ministry. This does not mean that your work will always be easy, that you will never want to do something else, or will never need a break. But learning to enjoy work is a means of keeping our eyes fixed on God's providence in our lives at present and making the most of what we have.

There is a danger here of keeping our eyes on the horizon and always looking for something better. The apostle James warned,

> Go to now, ye that say, To day or to morrow we will go into such a city, and continue there a year, and buy and sell, and get gain: whereas ye know not what shall be on the morrow. For what is your life? It is even a vapour, that appeareth for a little time, and then vanisheth away. For that ye ought to say, If the Lord will, we shall live, and do this, or that. (James 4:13–15)

We cannot assume that our plans will come to pass. The present may be all that we have to use to redeem the time. I know a man who longs to get a PhD and gain prestige by teaching at an academic institution. In the meantime, he cannot hold down a regular job and support his family. The days are evil. Satan would tempt you to keep your eyes on the horizon at the expense of the present. You can have godly reasons for wanting to change your career path, but never forget to be committed to serving the Lord today. Learn to enjoy your work and redeem the time.

Keep the Sabbath Holy

It is always more profitable to keep the Sabbath holy than it is to trample and profane the day (Isa. 58:13–14).[5] This takes one-seventh of your time. This direction is not a suggestion. It is one of the Ten Commandments. God made the Sabbath for man at creation, and the Sabbath continues as a pledge of entering into our heavenly rest until the day that we set foot safely on heaven's shores. A close friend frequently says that the Lord always gives us enough time to do what He calls us to do. Does God call us to break one of His commandments in order to

---

5. For reasons why the Lord's Day, or Sunday, is the Christian Sabbath and why we should keep it, see Joseph A. Pipa Jr., *The Lord's Day* (Geanies House, U.K.: Christian Focus, 1997). For expanded arguments regarding why and how to keep the entire day holy to the worship of God, see Ryan M. McGraw, *The Day of Worship: Reassessing the Christian Life in Light of the Sabbath* (Grand Rapids: Reformation Heritage Books, 2011).

fulfill others? Does He command us to redeem the time by working on the Sabbath while He simultaneously sets apart one-seventh of our time exclusively for His worship and service? God may have called you to be a student, but has He called you to study at the expense of worship and fellowship on the Lord's Day?

It is beyond the scope of this booklet to treat what is necessary on the Sabbath and what violates the purpose of the day. The important matter here is to search our hearts. Most excuses for breaking the Sabbath betray a lack of trust in the providence of God to bless our time working the other six days. Trust in the Lord of the Sabbath to give you the time to keep the Sabbath. Trust His command to keep it holy above your reasons for profaning it. We must redeem the time by Sabbath keeping because the Sabbath is, above all other time, redeemed time. It is the day on which Christ rose from the dead and gained victory over death for Himself and for us. It is the day that reminds us that there still remains a Sabbath rest for the people of God in heaven (Heb. 4:9). Let us be diligent to enter that rest (Heb. 4:11). Let us redeem the time by keeping the Sabbath day holy.

Always Prioritize Family
While we may include our families in our everyday tasks in life, this cannot replace the time that we spend with them directly. Husbands must take time to talk to their wives alone and to cultivate

their relationship with them if they would have strong marriages. In addition to family worship, catechizing, church, and education, parents need to take time to play with small children and communicate well with older children. Family vacations are a vital aspect of using our time well to the glory of the triune God. It is particularly offensive when men preface published PhD theses by noting that they have neglected their families in the process and intend to do better from now on. This is a sacrifice that is not worth making.

This is true with regard to men who sink themselves into other forms of work to the neglect of their families as well. One of the greatest tragedies that I have heard of was a man whose wife worked while homeschooling their children so that he could go to seminary full time. It is easy to justify this practice in the name of serving the church through the ministry. However, after a few years, his wife decided that if this was what the ministry entailed, then she had had enough. She left him in the middle of his studies, and he could neither complete his course at the seminary nor enter into the ministry. Regardless of your calling, you must designate regular time that belongs to your family alone. This is not losing time, but investing time well. Ministering to your family is integral to living a Spirit-filled life. It honors God by obeying His commands through loving family members in Christ. Prioritizing family is a good use of time and makes the days of our sojourning pleasant and happy.

Repent and Regroup

Question 87 of the Westminster Shorter Catechism is one of the best descriptions of the Christian life ever written: "Repentance unto life is a saving grace, whereby a sinner, out of a true sense of his sin, and apprehension of the mercy of God in Christ, doth, with grief and hatred of his sin, turn from it unto God, with full purpose of, and endeavor after, new obedience." Your best efforts to redeem the time will fail. You have not yet arrived in heaven; you are not yet made perfect in holiness. Those who use time well will sometimes become obsessed with time to their own detriment and often to the annoyance of those around them. Those who neglect their use of time become unproductive and frustrated, but they rarely like the alternative of being intentional with time.

Since we can never live perfectly in this life, does this mean that we should give up? No, we must repent and regroup. You will never be perfect in this life, but do you not desire to be perfect as your Father in heaven is perfect (Matt. 5:48)? What we call "perfectionism" is usually a form of pride in which we either want to think well of ourselves or want others to think well of us. Redeeming the time is a matter of love to God in Christ. The love of Christ must constrain us to live no longer for ourselves but for Him who died for us and rose from the dead (2 Cor. 5:14–15). Redeeming the time involves continual repentance.

We must recognize both that abusing time and wasting time are sin. Do you have a true sense of this sin—namely, that it is against the love of a heavenly Father? Do you apprehend, or lay hold of, the mercies of God in Christ? Do you flee to Him in light of your sin rather than run from Him into darkness? Do you grieve over and hate your sin because your sin grieves the Holy Spirit and because God hates your sin? Is it your full purpose to endeavor after new obedience? Have you been unintentional with your use of time, and have you lost sight of your priorities? Then lay hold of Christ and recover them. Have you become obsessed with overscheduling time, become discouraged with your work, and stopped enjoying your work to the glory of God? Then rest in Christ, who is your righteousness and who gives dignity to your work. Trust in the Spirit, who enables you to keep walking forward. Have you neglected the Sabbath and your family in the name of working hard and not being able to spare time for either of them? Confess your lack of trust in the God who is the Lord of time and whose Spirit alone enables you to redeem the time.

Repentance is a joyful duty and a beautiful grace in a Christian. Repentance means that God has already accepted your person in Christ, and now, through His grace, He will accept your works in

Christ. He will establish peace for you, for He has done all your works for you (Isa. 26:12). Through the grace of God at work in repentance, the Christian walk and life can always move forward. This is walking with God. It is a good path in which He leads us beside still waters (Ps. 23:2). He will lead you in paths of righteousness for His name's sake (Ps. 23:3). Repent, regroup, be of good cheer, and redeem the time.

CONCLUSION

Time is one of our most precious resources. Your life consists of time and you are not your own, but you have been bought with a price (1 Cor. 6:20). Seek to redeem the time, because the days are evil. View time management as a means of honoring the triune God and serving others. A schedule is a servant, not a master. Use time management as a means of managing your home and ministering to your local church. Worship the triune God who is the Lord and maker of time. Love the Father for choosing you in Christ before time began. Love and serve Christ for coming in the fullness of time to live, obey, suffer, die, and rise for your sake. Love the Spirit for enabling you to redeem the time. Time is the primary means that God has given you to glorify and to enjoy Him. To the Christian, time is full of opportunity. As we glorify the triune God by redeeming the time now, let us press onward cheerfully and thankfully, that we plan to do so forever.